The Library at the End of the World
by Brennan & White

www.brennanandwhite.com
@brennanandwhite

Published by Ignition Arts.
1st Ed. March 1, 2026

Inspired
Lists
Of
Valuable
Efforts
Yield
Open
Understanding

## CHARACTERS

CASSANDRA - desperate for someone to listen
MORIMOTO - needs a break
VAN GOGH - wants a life of art
SOLOMON - needs freedom
GOODY PROCTOR - searching for truth
MARINA AMBRAMOVIĆ - trying to be present
PHINEAS GAGE - trying to remember
JOSEPHINE BAKER - needs to communicate
FRANZ REICHELT – desperate to share
WILD CHILD– dealing with a lot of rage

## NOTE ON THE CHARACTERS

*All characters are open age, gender, and ethnicity. The names of the characters are the titles of their monologues; the titles are not people, but concepts.*

## SETTING

A Library

## NOTE ON THE TEXT

*Spacing, returns and capitalization are intentional. Go with the feel. Thoughts are interrupted, meander and wend. <> is an expression.*
*Throughout the piece, there are "tremors" during which stacks shake and books fall. This happens many times throughout the show, so pace yourself. Orchestrate this artistically however serves your ensemble.*
*There are many books.* ***THE book*** *is special.*

*The Library at the End of the World premiered with Montgomery County Community College on April 23, 2026 under the direction of Tim Gallagher. The opening night cast included:*

CASSANDRA - Patrick Kovach
MORIMOTO - Alex Voss
VAN GOGH - Autumn Sherry
SOLOMON - Juleon Gibson
GOODY PROCTOR - Star Gies
MARINA AMBRAMOVIĆ - Nayla Garcia
PHINEAS GAGE - Harris Betz
JOSEPHINE BAKER - Chrissy McGuinness
FRANZ REICHELT – Peyton Seitzinger
WILD CHILD – Persephone Harshbarger

Director: Tim Gallagher
Stage Manager: Elizabeth Kieser
Assistant Director: Will Olsen
Assistant Stage Manager:Erin Armstrong
Assistant Technical Director: Autumn Sherry
Set Designer: Rhea Khilnani
Properties Designer: Echo Wallower
Scenic Charge: Erin Armstrong
Costume/Hair/Makeup Designer: Persephone Harshbarger
Lighting Designer: Elizabeth Kieser
Sound Designer: Lia Cox
Stage Crew:
Michael Adamski, Lucca Brown, Peyton Seitzinger

## PRELUDE

*Darkness.*
*Music.*
*Lights up on Cassandra.*
*Cassandra holds a book.*
*Music swells then drops to a pinprick.*
*Cassandra opens the book.*
*Josephine starts their monologue, then Van Gogh, then Morimoto, Goody Proctor, Wild Child, Solomon, Phineas Gage, Franz, Marina.*

*It becomes a cacophony of text,*
*a waterfall of monologues.*
*After all of the characters have joined,*
*Cassandra calls above the throng:*

CASSANDRA

Listen to me! Listen to me!

*The characters abruptly freeze.*

CASSANDRA (cont.)

I am telling you
**I am telling you** what is going to happen if this continues
It's
Not
Going
To end
Well

For Anyone

*A book falls from the shelf; all look sharply.*

And the worst part is:
You're not going to believe me

*A tremor begins.*

*Cassandra closes the book.*
*The stacks shake, more books fall.*
*A whorl of movement.*
*All characters disappear save Josephine Baker.*
*Cassandra hides THE book in the stacks*
*& disappears.*
*Josephine sees.*

*The tremor ends.*

*Josephine Baker is the only one left.*

THE BEGINNING

*Once the coast is clear,*
*Josephine rushes to the book.*
*Josephine opens it.*
*The monologues whisper from the book.*

JOSEPHINE BAKER

*(reads)*

"Inspired lists of valuable efforts yields open understanding."

"Inspired
Lists
Of
Valuable
Efforts
Yields
Open
Understanding."
What –
What does that mean?

*The monologues emanating from the book swell. Sound from off. Josephine startles. Drops the book. Josephine disappears. PHINEAS GAGE ploughs in with a stack of books to reshelve.*

PHINEAS GAGE (PSYCHOLOGY BF 1-990)

<>
Oh.
Oh. Wait -
Why did I –
Why -

*Phineas drops the books and accidentally grabs THE book while picking them up.*

UH!
I came in here for something.

I know I –
<uhhhhhh>
This is so frustrating. It happens to me all the time.
Literally. All the time.
I was - I was out there and I came in here tooooooo....
I'll remember. I'll re- I'll go back out and -
<!!!!!>
It's like the harder I try to remember
The more I can't remember.
<growl>

*Phineas exits, with THE book.*
*Cassandra re-enters. Returns to the THE book.*
*Uh oh.*

CASSANDRA

Oh no.
Oh no.
Oh nonononononononononono
What was I thinking?
Who hides a book in a library?
Stupidstupidstupid

*Franz enters.*

FRANZ

Can I help you?

CASSANDRA

No one can help me.

*Continues searching.*

FRANZ

That's dire.

Maybe I can help.
What are you looking for?

CASSANDRA

A book.

FRANZ

Could you
be more
specific?

CASSANDRA

I cannot.

FRANZ

Is the book…Psychology?

CASSANDRA

I don't know.

FRANZ

Memoir?

CASSANDRA

I don't know.

FRANZ

Art History?

CASSANDRA

I don't know.

FRANZ

Parenting?

CASSANDRA

I don't know.

FRANZ

Design?

CASSANDRA

I don't know.

FRANZ

Arts & Architecture?

CASSANDRA

I don't know.

FRANZ

Performance Art?

CASSANDRA

I don't know.

FRANZ

Perhaps you remember the color of the cover?
Or the *size* of the book.

CASSANDRA

Why are you still talking?

FRANZ

I'm trying to help. Perhaps you recall the content of the material?

CASSANDRA

You wouldn't understand.

FRANZ

Arts & Crafts? Is it about making something? Making something beautiful and risky, something so risky in fact,
that if you show it to anyone you will literally
Die?

*This shifts something in Franz.*
*It's personal.*

CASSANDRA

What are you talking about?

FRANZ

Just an example. One of many. Chosen at random to illustrate a point.

CASSANDRA

Are you even a librarian?

FRANZ

Define "librarian."

CASSANDRA

Are you pretending to work here?

FRANZ

I'm asking if you need help.

CASSANDRA

I do need help!

FRANZ

And I am trying to help you. But apparently I can't even do that right.

*Franz begins to hyperventilate.*

CASSANDRA

What is going on?

FRANZ

*(Continues to panic.)*

Which tracks, really. It definitely tracks.

CASSANDRA

Okay. Take it easy. Deep breaths. Let's not cause a scene.

FRANZ

I'm just trying to help.

CASSANDRA

Okay okay you can help! Calm down.

FRANZ

*(Continued heavy breathing.)*

I thought that
You know
When you are having a rough time
Don't they say
It's best to reach out to help someone else
Right
Don't they say that?
Doesn't someone say that?

CASSANDRA

You're okay. It will be okay.

FRANZ

Do you really think so?

CASSANDRA

No.

FRANZ

What?

CASSANDRA

No, I don't think it will be okay.

FRANZ

Then why did you say that?

CASSANDRA

Isn't that just something people say so they don't completely give up? Like, yes, the dog is gonna die, but we all say he's gonna be okay because, I mean, what else is there?

FRANZ

Oh God, I knew it. Something is wrong.

CASSANDRA

One hundred percent. Something is definitely wrong.

FRANZ

Oh thank goodness.

CASSANDRA

You can help me. There's a book. I'm looking for a book. It's important. It was here but now it's gone.

FRANZ

We are in a library. There's nothing but books!
It's hopeless. We might as well just bury ourselves in Kafka and wait for death.

CASSANDRA

Get it together! You said you wanna help - So Help.

FRANZ

But I feel so helpless.

CASSANDRA
(GREEK MYTHOLOGY BL 780-820)

Listen to me! Listen to me!

FRANZ

Why?

CASSANDRA

It's like I'm - Oh, whatshername
You know, from that -
The Greeks! The Greek show!

You know where they all, they all die and marry their parents and don't listen to the prophets even though, even though the prophets come and say, *Such and such is going to happen!* And they are all, *oh, what? foolish old man, go back to your cave and your Sodoku, I would never kill my father and marry my mother*, and the prophet is like, *No, really, listen to me, king of all the land, you've displeased the gods and you are going to be punished* and they are all like, *let's drink wine and be merry, meet my wife-mother and my children-siblings.*

I mean, <>
that one wasn't the right story - that was
That was the other guy - *<trying to remember>*
...Ed. Ed-iiiii
It doesn't matter

<!> Cassandra! I'm Cassandra!
Cassandra is a prophet, see?
And she is condemned to Spout prophecies about
Future Catastrophes
But No One Believes her

That's me

It's supposed to be a *gift*
You know how it happened?
I'll tell you how it happened.

Because Apollo is all, *I love you Cassandra, I love you*
*and I'll love you forever!*
*or until I tire of your mortalness! I want to shower you*
*with gifts that you don't want and never asked for! Poof!*
*Now you can predict the future! You're welcome!*

and Cassandra is like,
*Oh,*
*wow,*
*thanks Apollo…*
…
*Loooooook. You are really special, like,*
*you are a reeeeeally special*
*god,*
*but I am just…. not that… into you?*
*Like that. I mean: I like you.*
*I mean, I love you of course, i love you, you are a god*
*and I love all the gods, mostly out of fear, but out of*
*devotion too, because duh, and I mean, let's not*

*discount the elephant in the room that there is this kinda*
*HUGE power dynamic we are not acknowledging in this*
*situation in that I'm mortal and going to Die - I could tell*
*you in fact how that will happen now that I can predict*
*the future, thanks for that. - And You, - you are this, um,*
*Eternal All Powerful God, so it's like -*
*have you heard about power dynamics in your, um,*
*many travels?*

And Apollo is like, *Why aren't you bowing down to me,*
*mortal, and kissing my godly feet?*

And Cassandra is all, *Apollo, It's not you; it's me.*

And Apollo is all like, *HARLOT! I SPIT IN YOUR MOUTH*
*AND NOW YOU ARE CURSED FOREVER!*

That's me
I'm cursed

And I am telling you
I am telling you what is going to happen if this
continues
It's
Not
Going
To end
Well

For Anyone

And the worst part is:
You're not going to believe me

FRANZ

What if-
What if I believe you?

CASSANDRA

You do?

FRANZ

Yes.
It will be okay.

CASSANDRA

Are you just saying that even though you know it's not the most likely outcome?

FRANZ

Yes.

CASSANDRA

Okay.

It will be okay.

FRANZ

I want to show you something.

*They exit together.*

*Phineas re-enters still holding a stack of books including THE book.*

PHINEAS GAGE

I didn't remember.
In case you were wondering
I mean.
Maybe I'm here to do this. *(indicating books to reshelve)*
I dunno.

*Phineas reshelves books during the following.*

I've been getting that sense lately.
That I'm looking for something. Always looking - onto the next thing, something better, something more interesting, more, I don't know. I don't know what it is. I never know what it is.

I wander into bookstores, libraries and I think -
maybe there's a secret -
Like a secret book
That has the answers.
I mean, how could we have come this far - you know, all this *evolution*
How could people have been alive this long and we still don't have any answers?!
Do you know there are things we still don't know about the brain? The brain! We all have one. I mean,
Ostensibly.
Some more than others it seems.
And we don't fully understand how it works.
You know Phineas Gage?

He-
This is the 1800s, mid 1800s.
He was working on - I dunno, mining or no- rock-
splitting? Is that a thing? Rock-spliting?
He was doing physical labor - in Vermont
And he had to, uh,
Fill this hole with gunpowder.
This is probably before unions
Or
Common sense, I dunno
Gage was a good guy, apparently, a real leader, even
keel, good worker, respectful

Well, he shoves the gunpowder in the hole and the pole
creates sparks and lights the gunpowder and
> B o o m <
Explodes
Shoots him back, a rod

Through    his    skull

He's a goner, of course, they all think
But minutes later, he is up and talking.

Talking.

And yes, he lost an eye - I don't want to get into it -
And he had all these surgeries, recovery, the works,
But he was still functional in every way

Except

Except
he became an asshole

Rude, swearing, poor work ethic
*He's not himself*, everyone said

And they Fired him! After he got a pole through his skull on the job!

Talk about a bum deal.

He -
I think he moved to Chile, worked another job
Ended up redeeming himself
Becoming less of a jerk, regaining his
Personality

He remembered things
With a rod through his skull

*Phineas has reshelved all books save THE book.*
*Phineas sits, absently palming THE book.*

I'm just gonna sit here and wait
Maybe it'll come to me

*MORIMOTO enters with a stack of books and starts to reshelve them.*

MORIMOTO

<Sigh>

<SIIIIGGGHHHGROOooooan…>

<SIIIIGGGHHHHHGROOOOOOOOOOAAAAAN…>

PHINEAS

Are you
Okay?

MORIMOTO

I need a break
From this
From All of This

PHINEAS

Do you, uh
work here?

MORIMOTO

Not a Vacation
Not a Day Off
A BREAK

PHINEAS

I hear you.

MORIMOTO

What are you doing?

PHINEAS

I'm looking for something.

MORIMOTO

You don't look like you are looking for anything.

PHINEAS

Well.
It's sort of a passive looking
It's sort of a trying to remember what I'm looking for looking.

MORIMOTO

Lemme help.

*Morimoto abandons the reshelving and starts searching the stacks for Phineas.*

PHINEAS

I thought you needed a break.

MORIMOTO

Can't take a break when there is work to be done.

PHINEAS

Could be why you are so exhausted.

MORIMOTO

I've got a knack for finding things.

PHINEAS

How do you know what I'm looking for
When I don't even know what I'm looking for?

MORIMOTO

I'll know it when I find it.
Sometimes you need someone else to find it
First

PHINEAS

And when you find it,
You'll let me know?

MORIMOTO

Yep.
It's all gonna be okay.

PHINEAS

I can't find anything. Not my keys, my bag, my glasses.
I can
Never remember where I parked. Or
Or people's names at parties
Or information
Information I'm supposed to know
Like
my Doctor's name or
Or Dates or Directions or Details

My mom
My mom just told me we had a party for all these
people
And I was There
I was THERE at the Party
And I have literally No Recollection of it
...

Do you think there's something wrong with me?

MORIMOTO

Maybe it's not that we forget,
Maybe we just can't recall the information at any given time.

PHINEAS

What does that mean?

MORIMOTO

It'll be okay.

PHINEAS

Do you think so?

MORIMOTO

What'd you say?

*Morimoto continues to comb through the stacks.*

PHINEAS

There's this woman
Doctors called her AJ
She can remember everything, Everything from her life.
But she didn't do well in school
She couldn't remember history or poetry
But her own life, she could remember. Every single detail.
She says she can feel Tuesday and Thursday and how they are different

She can pull dates from the card catalogue of her mind
And tell you everything that happened on. that. day.
And this other woman, - she's Australian-
She can quote every line in the *Harry Potter* series. There are over a MILLION WORDS in those books. She didn't memorize it. She just *knows* it.
You can give her a chapter number, and she'll tell you the title and the text. Her first memory was when she was 12 days old
They have HSAM - highly superior autobiographical memory
And I can't.
I can't even remember why I came into the room.

MORIMOTO

Well, that's everything. And if it's not here, it's-

*Clocks THE book Phineas is holding.*

Wait.

PHINEAS

What?

MORIMOTO

*Grabs THE book from Phineas and pages through.*

Is this-
Have you had this the whole time? Seriously?!
Oh.
Oh *WOW*.

PHINEAS

*Goes after the book.*

What? What is it?

MORIMOTO

*Continues to page through.*

Oh, this is -

PHINEAS

Can I-
Can I see it please?!

MORIMOTO

I just looked through everything and
You've had this THE WHOLE TIME.

*Phineas grabs the book back.*

PHINEAS

This is - how -
this is what I was looking for-
How did you know?

MORIMOTO

Well. Because
I guess
I guess I needed it too.

*They read together.*
*Then Morimoto takes off into the monologue.*

PHINEAS & MORIMOTO

I need a break
From this
From All of This

Not a Vacation
Not a Day Off
A BREAK

PHINEAS

I don't-
I don't
understand.

*Throughout Morimoto's monologue,*
*Phineas sometimes reads along and joins,*
*baffled by the circumstance.*

MORIMOTO
(MEMOIR CT 21-183)

I just wanna-

Go to the Woods
And hole up
in a little
I dunno
Snow-covered cottage
And sit by the fire
And maybe
Drink tea or or
hot chocolate

Or Soup
Make soup
And
NOTHING ELSE
Nothing
Just like
Look at the fire
Me cottage snow hot chocolate soup fire
NOTHING ELSE

Or like-

Sit in a hammock
L a y in a hammock
by a stream
I mean, if it's nice out
In the woods
>I feel like I need to go to the woods<
And just
Read
Or
Not Read
Just Listen to the stream
And Let the Messages from the Universe come
Just l a y there
And let my mind w a n d e r
And not worry about things like
Like like like

"Tomorrow and tomorrow and tomorrow
Creeps in this petty pace from day to day
To the last syllable of recorded time;

And all our yesterdays have lighted fools
The way to dusty death."
Just me hammock stream book – no book – Universe,
t h o u g h t s

And NOTHING

<...>
I've been having this dream
Where i- i'm driving a car
And i'm speeding toward a bridge, but the bridge is
only partially complete
it's-It's just half a bridge
Or
or I'm taking a curve of a winding road too fast
And it's a plummet
A straight drop
No guardrails at the turn
Just DESCENT
And I'm going too fast, I know I'm going to fast
And I'm always driving someone - it's never just me
There's always someone else in the car too
And I know I'm
Responsible for
For sending us off this cliff
And I'm pulling on the wheel and pulling on the wheel
and the car is skidding
And we're Off
Off the edge
And there is          n   o   t   h   i   n   g
Nothing but air

And in that moment
I know it's all my fault
And I know there's no going back
And I have to come to terms with everything
Everything
i have ever done and not done
And I feel
<It's weird>
But I feel

at peace

Because
I have to be
there's no other choice
And if you have to choose,
I mean
Isn't it better to choose
peace?

<...>
There is this guy
I don't know why I thought of this-
In Japan
-This is true-
There is this guy in Japan who rents himself out
To do nothing
He accompanies people, pretends to be a family member or a date or whatever
But he also just-

Sometimes he just sits with people and reads Manga
while they work
Says goodbye to them on a train platform, takes a walk
with them in the park
And

I kinda wanna do that
Maybe not forever
But it'd be nice
If
I dunno
If I didn't have to -
If I could
Just
Be here
With someone
And
Just be me

*Phineas has been holding the book the whole time, grappling with the text inside and the text aloud.*

PHINEAS

(re: *the book*) But this is. This is just-

MORIMOTO

What?

PHINEAS

Text.

MORIMOTO

So?

PHINEAS

There are no...
THERE ARE NO ANSWERS!
I WAS LOOKING FOR ANSWERS!
Answers in a secret book - small, leatherbound
preferably,
old-looking, maybe bejeweled.
I don't know: Gilded. I would open it up and things
would be *REVEALED*
THINGS WOULD *CHANGE*

MORIMOTO

Things have changed. Don't you get it?
<>
I spoke.

PHINEAS

And?

MORIMOTO

And
you listened.

And now
we don't need the book.

*Morimoto takes Phineas off.*
*They leave the book.*

*A tremor. Books fall.*

*Lights rise on SOLOMON & VAN GOGH.*
*They have been considering the book for a long time.*

VAN GOGH

This is ridiculous!

SOLOMON

It's not so bad.

VAN GOGH

It's preposterous!

SOLOMON

It could be worse.

VAN GOGH

It could be worse?!?!

There are
no answers here -
We have been looking forever
How long have we been looking?

SOLOMON

Forever.
We have been looking forever.
And I feel like if we don't find it -
Something /horrible will happen.

VAN GOGH

/Something horrible will happen. You said, yes.

SOLOMON

<sigh>
It will be okay.

VAN GOGH

Are you just saying that or do you actually believe it?

SOLOMON

It has to be said.

VAN GOGH

And this is-
Are you sure this is it?

*Solomon takes the book and reads.*

SOLOMON

"Inspired lists of valuable -"

VAN GOGH

I know I know

SOLOMON

It's the correct inscription.

VAN GOGH

This is just a collection of words on a page.

SOLOMON

What were you expecting?

VAN GOGH

Something
More
I dunno
Answers! I thought we'd get answers.
Why else are we here?

SOLOMON

Maybe we have to -
Never mind.

VAN GOGH

What?

SOLOMON

Nothing.

VAN GOGH

Say it.

SOLOMON

Maybe we have to
Think about it.

VAN GOGH

Think about what?

SOLOMON

"Inspired Lists of Valuable Efforts Yield Open Understanding."

VAN GOGH

Yadda yadda yadda.

SOLOMON

It could be important.

VAN GOGH

Doesn't seem like much of an answer.

SOLOMON

Maybe it's not about answers.
Maybe it's about art.

VAN GOGH

Art? I'm sorry.
Did you say
Art?

SOLOMON

Yes, Art.
Maybe art is the answer.

VAN GOGH
(ART HISTORY NX 440-632)

People don't want *art*!

They want product
and plastic

And propaganda

They want
-I dunno -
Cheap Home Renovations
And Parenting Hacks
and Muffin Recipes with Hidden Nutrients
And
and Storage Ideas for Small Spaces
and Muddy Toddlers Carrying Inappropriate Animals in from Outdoors:
    *What's that, sweetie? A squirrel, a gopher, a baby skunk?*
    *Oh, isn't he darling?*

Or they don't
They don't know *what* they want
And so they search and they search and they search,
but what they are searching for
Is
Already there
It's *inside*
*Inside them*
And it's rotting
It's rotting with
Every. single. moment. they are ignoring it
And feeding it Drek

And when they stop
When they stop the endless treadmill of
JUNK

You know what they stop on?

In a world of Big Thinkers
Of Incredible Creators
And Masters of Craft and Form and Skill
Of Linguists and Maestros
Of Virtuosos and Sages?

A hamster video
It's a hamster
Inside a cardboard box

It's elaborate
I mean, it's an elaborate hamster set up

It's an *Indiana-Jones*-level set up
With cardboard boxes
Like ALL the cardboard boxes
-Possibly ever created

And the little hamster is wiggling his little nose
And he's gotta get through this maze
And there's music:
Like <sings dangerous music>
<dangerous music starts>
<becomes the hamster>

And it starts simple enough
He has to weave through passages,
Slip through a slinky

There are little matchstick barricades
- and straws
He's gotta duck and jump over straws and pipe cleaners
And then it gets harder
There are levels, see?
Pringles containers to sneak through
And crumpled cut up paper
He lands in little vats of stuff, like
Ball pits of paper
and has to claw his way out

At one point there are these little blue styrofoam balls
They pour out of a hole in the maze wall and he sneaks inside the hole
And then you can see, he's like
*Oh shit*
*Bad idea*
And he comes right out
And it's like:
We're on the Titanic

*<Music shifts.>*

And the water is coming in
The water is pouring out of the hole
He's gotta get out
And he's eating -
I think he eats some of the styrofoam to get out
Or by mistake
I don't know what he's thinking at this point

But I'm thinking:
*Is this fun?*
*Was he ever having fun?*
*What am I watching?*

And then things get real:
Like <sings scarier music, like Carmina Burana>
The maze starts to move
There are blades covered in Blood
And like
Spiky things coming outta nowhere
Moving walls
If he had a tail
His tail woulda been cut off by now from the moving walls

And yeah it's all cardboard and toothpicks and nail polish
But HE doesn't know that
He's all
<Scamper scamper>
His little nose working the whole time
His little claw feet navigating falling bridges
And tunnels with like
plastic spiders the size half dollars
And decoupaged Dead bodies
And rotting rubber skeletons

And every time you think, *he's made it!*
*He must be done!*
There is Another level

He's always Leveling up
The music is always getting more stressful and terrifying
I mean
*Are they gonna feed him to a cat at the end or something?!*

WE DON'T KNOW
ANYTHING COULD HAPPEN
WHAT AM I DOING WITH MY LIFE

And i realize:
I AM THE HAMSTER
I have ALWAYS BEEN THE HAMSTER
I am always leveling up
But instead of things getting easier
They get harder
The game gets more complicated, more dangerous
There are Spikes and falling Objects and Monsters on all sides
>Are the monsters real? I don't know. It sure FEELS like they are.<
And the music keeps getting
WORSE

*Music cuts out.*
*Sudden silence.*
*Stillness.*

When Van Gogh painted sunflowers, no one was interested.

When he was institutionalized, he created "Starry Night" from the nighttime view from his asylum window.

He only sold one painting during his lifetime
and died poor.

127 million people have seen that hamster navigate a cardboard maze.

Do you still think they really want art?

SOLOMON
I don't know what they want.

VAN GOGH
You can't have the book.

SOLOMON
What makes you think I even want the book?

VAN GOGH
You shouldn't have the book.

SOLOMON
What are you talking about?

VAN GOGH
Please. I know you. You are searching for all the answers so you can keep them to yourself.

SOLOMON

But we don't even know
What the answer is!

VAN GOGH

That's how these things go. That's how they've always gone. Someone finds something...an answer, a hint, a clue, a suggestion... and they hide it so no one else can see it.

Give me the book.

SOLOMON

But you don't want the book.

It's
You know,
Art.

VAN GOGH

Hand it over.

SOLOMON

I don't want to.

VAN GOGH

Of course not. You want to be the only person in the world who knows what's in the book.

SOLOMON

That's ridiculous.

We can Both have the book.

VAN GOGH

You say that now.
But if you find the answer,
You'll keep it to yourself.

SOLOMON
(PARENTING HQ 755.7 - 755.92)

No I won't. That's you.
I'm not like you.

VAN GOGH

No?

SOLOMON

Not really.
A little bit, maybe.

VAN GOGH

Ah-ha!

SOLOMON

Sometimes it feels like I *am* you.
And there's no other choice
It's predestined
Preordained:
    I will become you
But I-
I don't want to be like you.
Not that there's anything wrong with you.

It's just that there are so many things that are wrong with
you.
You know who you are?
You're Abraham.
In the Bible.
Ever read it?
Me neither.
But the story goes that God tells Abraham to cut his son
in half. And Abraham is like,
*Word up, God! Bet!*
And he is ready to cut his son in half but then God is like
*Whoa, dude! I wasn't serious. That was just a test to see
if you were a jerk and guess what... you are.*
Or. Wait. That-
That story might have been about Devotion.
I think it was the other -
The other story about the king and the people arguing
about a baby
Yes, yes.

There were these two women
Arguing that a baby was their baby, right?
And they go to the king
And the king, in all his wisdom, says *Okay, we'll just cut
him in half and you can each get half of the baby*
And the one mother is like, *Great idea, shared custody*!
But the *true* mother is like, *I will give him up to let him
live!*
And then the king - King Midas maybe?
But I don't think it was King Midas because he was the

one who turned everything to gold including his
daughter- *spoiler alert* - it did Not work out well for him
So then the King, who was noble and like the kind of king you want in charge, I mean, if you have to have a king,
SOLOMON!
It was King Solomon!
King Solomon says, *Mother who gave up the child so he could live, the child is clearly yours because you have his best intentions in mind - basically, not splitting him in twain.*
Seems like a low bar.
<> But maybe it's not.
You can't split everything in half
Not everything can break apart and still survive

*Picks up the book. Places it in front of Van Gogh.*

And some of us?
Some of us would rather let something go if it means it will live.

*Solomon exits, leaves Van Gogh with the book.*
*Franz enters.*

FRANZ REICHELT
(AVIATION TL 501-571)

I made a thing!
I made an amazing thing!
I made an amazing thing that no one has ever made before!
You are going to freak out at this thing I made!

It's a thing that I made and when you see it, It'll be like someone unscrewed the top of your head, blew on your brain, then screwed the top of your head back on again. That's how crazy the thing I made is!

*Pause.*

Do you want to see the thing?

*Pause.*

Do you?

*Van Gogh shrugs.*

Okay! I'm gonna go get the thing!

*Starts to exit.*

Are you sure you want to see the thing? It's a pretty awesome thing. I don't want your mind to be so blown by the thing that it causes permanent damage. So are you sure?

*Van Gogh reluctantly nods.*

Okay. I'm gonna go get the thing!

*Van Gogh gets an idea, pages through the book.*

*Finds THIS text inside the book.*

*Franz returns.*

*Van Gogh mouths some of the following text with Franz.*

FRANZ (cont).

I don't think you're ready to see the thing. I know what you're thinking! You're thinking "You didn't make a thing!" But that's not true! I made a thing! I thought about it! I imagined it, I figured out how to make it and I created the thing!

*When Franz approaches,*
*Van Gogh abruptly closes the book.*

Okay
To be honest,
I'm a little scared to show you the thing.

'Cause here's the thing about the thing.
It might not work, the thing. It might not.

It might be like a parachute suit. I mean…it's not a parachute suit. But -
Have you heard about the parachute suit?

VAN GOGH

From…Franz Reichelt?

FRANZ

Franz Reichelt, yes!

That's who built the parachute suit.
He was French. Lived in France.
He was a tailor. Fixed people's pants. Also built the parachute suit.
>This is real. This really happened.<
It was a suit for pilots that would turn into a parachute if they had to jump out of an airplane but didn't have time to put on a parachute. Not a bad idea. A little niche, but interesting, right?
They'd get into the air and it would turn into a parachute and they'd float effortlessly down to the ground.

But he had to test it. So he went to the police and he said "I have to test my thing!" And they said "How?" and he said "by jumping off the top of the Eiffel Tower!" And they said "Are you drunk?" but they said it in French so it was "Tu es bourrée?"

And Franz said "Non, je ne suis pas ivre," which is obviously French for "No, I'm not drunk!"

Franz wanted to show his thing to everyone! Then, finally, on February 4, 1912, he got permission to jump off the Eiffel Tower.
Really. He did.
This happened.

His friends tried to talk him out of it but Franz said "Don't try to talk me out of this, friends! I made this amazing thing and it's going to be beautiful." But he said it in French. Probably. I mean, I don't know.

So he went to the first platform of the Eiffel Tower wearing his parachute suit. You ever see the first platform? It's high. Higher than you are thinking. It's not a first anything. There were movie cameras. Hundreds of people gathered to watch Franz leap from the tower and float effortlessly to the ground.

And when you see the film, there's-
There's this moment in the film
where he's not sure if he should jump. You can tell he's thinking "What if I'm wrong? What if my thing is a failure?"

But Franz leapt.

Franz plummeted fifty-seven meters to the ground.
That's 187 feet.
That's approximately the height of a 16-story building.

The parachute didn't slow his descent at all. Not even a little.
There was a big poof of dust.
Franz died instantly.

*During Franz's monologue,*
*Van Gogh pages forward in the book*
*and sees that Franz will eventually*
*gain the courage to show the "thing"*
*if Van Gogh relinquishes the book.*

As you can imagine, it really cast a pall on the afternoon.
And when you know
when you Know what's going to happen, you want to yell, "Franz, don't jump! You'll die! Franz, ne saute pas, tu vas mourir!"

But no matter how many times you watch the film and wish he won't jump...Franz jumps.

What if
What if my thing is like a parachute suit?

*In response, Van Gogh slides the book to Franz.*
*Franz opens it and reads.*

FRANZ
"Inspired lists of valuable efforts yield open understanding."
I don't understand.

VAN GOGH
Maybe you don't have to.

*Van Gogh exits,*
*leaving Franz alone with the book.*

*WILD CHILD rushes on and makes A MESS,*
*raging and growling.*
*Franz is appropriately appalled.*

WILD CHILD
(SOCIOLOGY HM 1-1281)
I'M SO ANGRY.

FRANZ
Yeah
I - I got that.

WILD CHILD
But I don't
I don't want to be this way
I don't *wanna* be angry, don't you see?
I wanna be
Easy. I want everything to be
Easier. Everything feels like an emergency.
Doesn't everything feel like an emergency?!
Look at my eye
It's swollen, right? What Is That?
And my back
My back just started spasming outta nowhere today
Like it like it like it
Didn't want to be a part of me anymore
It wants OUT of my body
My body wants out of my body
It's all this
-Stress-
Stress isn't a big enough word

It's like, my body is manifesting all of the Emotional
Angst of the Entire World
And it's punishing me with it
It doesn't matter how well adjusted I try to be
Or how Pleasant I am
Or how Calmly I try to deal with
E V E R Y T H I N G
It's like
It's a – parasite – no, that's not the word
It's like
--an Infection
The Stress is an Infection and it's taking over my body
And now my body is Rebelling
And trying to get Out of my body
And I cannot help but DESTROY EVERYTHING
I wanna
I wanna
<howl>
<howl>
Oh wow, that feels good. Try it.

*FRANZ is hesitant.*

No really, try it.

*Franz tries a meager howl.*
*Then WILD CHILD howls, then Franz,*
*then back and forth until something is purged.*
*They stop.*

WILD CHILD (cont.)

Have you heard of the wild child?

Memie Le Blanc - The Wild Girl of Champagne.
She lived for ten years in the forest
Until she was captured by the villagers of Songy in 1731.
After raiding an apple orchard dressed in rags.
She actually fought the villagers with a large wooden club.
One of the village noblemen told a bunch of hunters
"Capture her!"
So they did.
There are interviews.
Biographies.
But none of them say whether or not her capture was a good thing

What if Memie was just fine in the forest?
Living with the animals.
Fighting with a club.
Raiding the orchards.

No one questions it.
Instead, they say "Memie still learned to read and write!"
She lived to be very old
She even became wealthy!

But what if that's not the point?
What if the point is just....(can't find the words)
<howl>

And there are others - Victor of Aveyron, Kamala &
Amala in India, Marina Chapman in Columbia.
There are children who were
Literally
raised by wolves.
Or animals. They survived in the wild. Alone.
Abandoned.
From infancy, some of them.
How did they -
<>
I know I'm not alone. Not exactly.
But I can't help but feel like no one is coming.
No one is coming to save us.

FRANZ

I read that rage isn't really an emotion.

WILD CHILD

Oh?

FRANZ

It's the feeling of injustice in disguise.

Can I show you something?

WILD CHILD

What if I break it?

FRANZ

I guess that's just a risk I'm going to have to take.

*Franz leads the Wild Child out.*
*Franz leaves the book.*
*A tremor. Books fall.*
*Josephine Baker appears. Scoops up the book.*

JOSEPHINE
(PERFORMING ARTS PN 1530-1590)
"Inspired lists of valuable efforts yield open
understanding."
What–
What does that mean?
"Inspired lists of valuable efforts yield open
understanding."

Do you know Josephine Baker?
Not personally, I mean,
-from history.
You probably know her from the banana skirt.
She took vaudeville by storm.
Born in St. Louis, became the toast of France.
1500 marriage proposals - that's what they say
She received 1500 marriage proposals.
Could you imagine?
She adopted children from all over the world - 12
12 children!
She called them her Rainbow Tribe
To show that people from all over the world could live
and grow together in peace
That's how she created her family.
And she-

During the war, the second world war
She smuggled messages for the French
through invisible ink in her sheet music
She sent messages in code.

Cause no one expects a performer to do anything but entertain

I think about her sometimes.
It's funny what we remember about a person.
She was the only woman to speak at the March on Washington in 1968
And she received the highest medal of honor for her service to the French during the war.
"Inspired lists of valuable efforts yield open understanding."
All people think of is the banana skirt.

*Goody Proctor enters somewhere during the previous monologue and listens.*

GOODY

That's flapdoodle.

JOSEPHINE

Pardon?

GOODY

FLAP-DOODLE, I say.
Marriage proposals? Sheet music? Codes?

JOSEPHINE

Codes! Yes, like when you read every other word.
Or substitute letters for numbers.
Or you only read the first letter of every word!

GOODY

Poppycock, balderdash, blatherskite.

JOSEPHINE

It's not. It's -

GOODY

Claptrap, codswallop, taradiddle.

JOSEPHINE

Who are you?

GOODY

Who are you?

JOSEPHINE

I
Well, I'm -

GOODY

You don't know, do you?
You stagger around,
avoiding falling books,
Eaves dropping on other people's stories
like it means something.

JOSEPHINE

It does mean something. I know it. I just don't know what.

GOODY

It means nothing.

JOSEPHINE

I know it will be okay.

*Goody Proctor picks up the book*
*and slams it into Josephine.*

GOODY PROCTOR (US HISTORY F 1-975)

It will be okay?!
People are being Murdered in the streets
Women dragged into Unmarked Cars
Taken away from their families
-Children-
The Elderly
I am afraid to come here
To this place
I am afraid to go anywhere
It's like my whole system is on high alert at all times
DINGDINGDINGDINGDING:
Dangerdangerdangerdanger

*Tremor. Books fall from shelves.*
*It's as if the library is part of Goody.*

I have to force myself to breathe

It's like my body forgets how

<deep breath in, out>

I was driving the other day
The other day i was driving along
And I saw this Lump on the side of the road
And I was like
"Ohmygod that's a dead body"
And it didn't phase me
I mean, it phased me but also
It was my first thought
Why was that my first thought?
    Oh, look, a lump on the side of the road:
    A dead body
...

It was a heap of trash

*Another tremor. More books fall from shelves.*

When they were burning witches
At the stake
Like in the 1600s
- No, sorry, -
I mean: women
When they were burning *women*
At the stake

They burned *women*
Not witches

It was dark, right? No electricity then
And people - they didn't have eye exams like we do
I mean, how many people do you know that wear glasses, right?
And so lots of people are stumbling around in the dark times
With poor eye sight
And so they saw things
In the dark
Plus the devil was Everywhere
I mean, not like a lot of entertainment options in the 1600s, you know
It was like...I dunno
Church and Executions and... Animal-baiting
So you could see why they'd be stressed out

*A larger tremor. More books fall.*

And there's that play
We read it in high school
The one with the, um, the
*"I saw Goody Proctor with the devil and I saw Goody Corey with the devil"*
And when i was reading that play
I was walking home from school
And I glanced down
And there was a dead crow under a tree
A dead crow
And I thought, *wow, it's everywhere*
*The devil* is *everywhere*

Then I did a double take:
It was just an old black work glove.

Something horrible is going to happen.
Something horrible is going to happen.

*Goody Proctor is distraught.*
*Books begin flying off the shelves. It is chaos.*

*MARINA AMBRAMOVIĆ enters.*

MARINA
(To Josephine Baker)

You can go.
I got this.

JOSEPHINE

"Inspired lists of valuable efforts yield open understanding."

*Josephine hands Marina the book.*

*The tremors begin to abate. Books stop falling.*

MARINA AMBRAMOVIĆ

Ah.
"Inspired lists of valuable efforts yield open understanding."

*Josephine leaves.*

*Marina gingerly pages through the book.*
*Marina addresses Goody Proctor.*

MARINA (PERFORMANCE ART NX 1-820)
You don't have to say anything.
You can just nod.

You don't even have to nod if you don't want to.
We can just be here with each other.
<....>
Sometimes
Sometimes I feel like I have to
Do something, say something, be somewhere
or it means that I'm not
I dunno.
Enough. I'm not Doing enough.
But that's not true.
I have to tell myself, everyday I have to
Remind myself: That's not true
And in time-
When I Don't do anything
Or Say anything or go anywhere
In time I realize
What is true
<...>

*Throughout the following, the other actors come out and sit across from each other in different configurations, mirroring Marina Ambramović's piece.*

There's this artist, you know her?
This, um, Yugoslavian artist
Who-
I don't think Yugoslavia exists anymore...
Well, she did this piece where she
She sat for eight hours a day
And made eye contact with strangers
When did she go to the bathroom I wonder
Or eat - Or
I mean it's not about that, but also these are the things I think about-
The point is
The point is:
people would sit for
Minutes
Hours
And just
<>
Three months, almost every day, eight hours a day
Over *700* hours
Of
Being
Present
...
What, has it been like,
a minute?
I think
It makes us uncomfortable.
The quiet.
<>

Sometimes I feel the weight of grief in my solar plexus
as if it's coming from inside me. Like it's the Nothing
and it's going to swallow me from the inside out,
transform me into something monstrous and savage,
until I don't recognize myself. Until I'm nothing but grief.
Sometimes I feel like I could cry until the end of time
and it wouldn't be enough.

*Goody picks up the book and reads.*

GOODY

"Inspired. Lists. Of. Valuable. Efforts. Yield. Open. Understanding."

*The remaining characters peel away from each other. Goody and Marina stay with each other.*

CASSANDRA

Listen to me.
Listen to me.

GOODY

It's a code.

*Music begins.*

FRANZ

I made a thing.

MARINA

It's a code.

FRANZ

I made an amazing thing.

MARINA

There are messages everywhere if you are willing to listen.

*A book ballet throughout the following collage of text.*

PHINEAS

I came in here looking for something.

GOODY

Inspired.

VAN GOGH

I am the hamster.
I have always been the hamster.

MARINA

Lists.

WILD CHILD

I don't want to be this way.
I don't want to be angry.

GOODY

Of.

SOLOMON

Sometimes it feels like there's no other choice.

MARINA

Valuable.

JOSEPHINE

To show how people from all over the world could live
and grow together in peace-

GOODY

Efforts.

JOSEPHINE

That's how she created her family.

MARINA

Yield.

CASSANDRA

Cassandra is a prophet, see?

GOODY

Open.

CASSANDRA

But no one believes

MARINA

Understanding.

GOODY

But
is that the answer?

FRANZ
Et si je me trompais? Et si j'échouais?

MARINA
Šta misliš? *("What do you think?" in Serbian)*

PHINEAS
It's sort of a passive looking
It's sort of a trying to remember what I'm looking for looking.

MARINA
Let's sit.

VAN GOGH
What am I doing with my life?

GOODY
Okay.

JOSEPHINE
It's funny what we remember about a person.

GOODY
And?

WILD CHILD
I know I'm not alone

MARINA
Let's be with one another.

MORIMOTO

Just let the messages from the universe come

MARINA

Can you feel it?

GOODY

What?

MARINA

The
Possibility.

*A swell of music.*
*The book ballet culminates*
*in a beautiful ascending moment of awe.*

END OF PLAY

www.ingramcontent.com/pod-product-compliance
Lightning Source LLC
LaVergne TN
LVHW091011080826
845145LV00003B/1227

* 9 7 8 1 9 6 6 0 0 4 1 2 7 *

The Library at the End of the World
by Brennan & White

The Monologues

## PHINEAS GAGE

<>

Oh.
Oh. Wait -
Why did I –
Why -

*PG drops the books and accidentally grabs THE book while picking them up.*

UH!
I came in here for something.
I know I –
<uhhhhhh>

This is so frustrating. It happens to me all the time.
Literally. All the time.
I was - I was out there and I came in here tooooooo....

I'll remember. I'll re- I'll go back out and -

<!!!!!>

It's like the harder I try to remember
The more I can't remember.

<growl>

*Exits, returns.*

I didn't remember.
In case you were wondering
I mean.

Maybe I'm here to do this. *(indicating books to reshelve)*
I dunno.

I've been getting that sense lately.
That I'm looking for something. Always looking - onto the next thing, something better, something more interesting, more, I don't know. I don't know what it is. I never know what it is.

I wander into bookstores, libraries and I think -
maybe there's a secret -
Like a secret book
That has the answers.
I mean, how could we have come this far - you know, all this evolution
How could people have been alive this long and we still don't have any answers?!

Do you know there are things we still don't know about the brain? The brain! We all have one. I mean,
Ostensibly.
Some more than others it seems.
And we don't fully understand how it works.

You know Phineas Gage?

He-

This is the 1800s, mid 1800s.
He was working on - I dunno, mining or no- rock-splitting? Is that a thing? Rock-spliting?
He was doing physical labor - in Vermont
And he had to, uh,
Fill this hole with gunpowder.
This is probably before unions
Or

Common sense, I dunno
Gage was a good guy, apparently, a real leader, even keel, good worker, respectful

Well, he shoves the gunpowder in the hole and the pole creates sparks and lights the gunpowder and
> B o o m <
Explodes
Shoots him back, a rod

Through his skull

He's a goner, of course, they all think
But minutes later, he is up and talking.

Talking.

And yes, he lost an eye - I don't want to get into it -
And he had all these surgeries, recovery, the works,
But he was still functional in every way

Except

Except
he became an asshole

Rude, swearing, poor work ethic
*He's not himself*, everyone said

And they Fired him! After he got a pole through his skull on the job!

Talk about a bum deal.

He -
I think he moved to Chile, worked another job
Ended up redeeming himself
Becoming less of a jerk, regaining his
Personality

He remembered things
With a rod through his skull

*Phineas has reshelved all books save THE book. Phineas sits, absently palming THE book.*
I'm just gonna sit here and wait
Maybe it'll come to me

...

I can't find anything. Not my keys, my bag, my glasses.
I can
Never remember where I parked. Or

Or people's names at parties
Or information
Information I'm supposed to know
Like
my Doctor's name or
Or Dates or Directions or Details

My mom
My mom just told me we had a party for all these people
And I was There
I was THERE at the Party
And I have literally No Recollection of it
...
Do you think there's something wrong with me?
There's this woman
Doctors called her AJ
She can remember everything, Everything from her life.
But she didn't do well in school
She couldn't remember history or poetry
But her own life, she could remember. Every single detail.

She says she can feel Tuesday and Thursday and how they are different
She can pull dates from the card catalogue of her mind
And tell you everything that happened on. that. day.

And this other woman, - she's Australian-

She can quote every line in the *Harry Potter* series. There are over a MILLION WORDS in those books. She didn't memorize it. She just *knows* it.

You can give her a chapter number, and she'll tell you the title and the text. Her first memory was when she was 12 days old

They have HSAM - highly superior autobiographical memory

And I can't.

I can't even remember why I came into the room.

## CASSANDRA

Listen to me! Listen to me!

It's like I'm - Oh, whatshername
You know, from that -
The Greeks! The Greek show!

You know where they all, they all die and marry their parents and don't listen to the prophets even though, even though the prophets come and say, *Such and such is going to happen*
And they are all, *oh, what? foolish old man, go back to your cave and your Sodoku, I would never kill my father and marry my mother*, and the prophet is like, *No, really, listen to me, king of all the land, you've displeased the gods and you are going to be punished* and they are all like, *let's drink wine and be merry, meet my wife-mother and my children-siblings.*

I mean, <>
that one wasn't the right story - that was
That was the other guy - *<trying to remember>*
...Ed. Ed-iiiii
It doesn't matter

<!>Cassandra! I'm Cassandra!
Cassandra is a prophet, see?
And she is condemned to Spout prophecies about
Future Catastrophes
But No One Believes her

That's me

It's supposed to be a *gift*
You know how it happened?
I'll tell you how it happened.

Because Apollo is all, *I love you Cassandra, I love you and I'll love you forever!*
*or until I tire of your mortalness! I want to shower you with gifts that you don't want and never asked for! Poof! Now you can predict the future! You're welcome!*

and Cassandra is like,
*Oh,*
*wow,*
*thanks Apollo…*
…
*Looooook. You are really special, like,*
*you are a reeeeeally special*
*god,*
*but I am just…. not that… into you?*
*Like that. I mean: I like you.*
*I mean, I love you of course, i love you, you are a god and I love all the gods, mostly out of fear, but out of devotion too, because duh, and I mean, let's not discount the elephant in the room that there is this kinda HUGE power dynamic we are not acknowledging in this situation in that I'm mortal and going to Die – I could tell you in fact how that will happen now that I can predict*

*the future, thanks for that. - And You, - you are this, um, Eternal All Powerful God, so it's like - have you heard about power dynamics in your, um, many travels?*

And Apollo is like, *Why aren't you bowing down to me, mortal, and kissing my godly feet?*

And Cassandra is all, *Apollo, It's not you; it's me.*

And Apollo is all like, *HARLOT! I SPIT IN YOUR MOUTH AND NOW YOU ARE CURSED FOREVER!*

That's me
I'm cursed

And I am telling you
**I am telling you** what is going to happen if this continues
It's
Not
Going
To end
Well

For Anyone

And the worst part is:
You're not going to believe me

MORIMOTO

I need a break
From this
From All of This

Not a Vacation
Not a Day Off
A BREAK

I just wanna-

Go to the Woods
And hole up
in a little
I dunno
Snow-covered cottage
And sit by the fire
And maybe
Drink tea or or
hot chocolate
Or Soup
Make soup
And
NOTHING ELSE
Nothing
Just like
Look at the fire
Me cottage snow hot chocolate soup fire
NOTHING ELSE

Or like-

Sit in a hammock
L a y in a hammock
by a stream
I mean, if it's nice out
In the woods
>I feel like I need to go to the woods<
And just
Read
Or
Not Read
Just Listen to the stream
And Let the Messages from the Universe come
Just l a y there
And let my mind w a n d e r
And not worry about things like
Like like like

> "Tomorrow and tomorrow and tomorrow
> Creeps in this petty pace from day to day
> To the last syllable of recorded time;
> And all our yesterdays have lighted fools
> The way to dusty death."

Just me hammock stream book - no book- Universe, t h o u g h t s

And NOTHING

<...>
I've been having this dream

Where i- i'm driving a car
And i'm speeding toward a bridge, but the bridge is only partially complete
it's-It's just half a bridge
Or
or I'm taking a curve of a winding road too fast
And it's a plummet
A straight drop
No guardrails at the turn
Just DESCENT
And I'm going too fast, I know I'm going to fast
And I'm always driving someone - it's never just me
There's always someone else in the car too
And I know I'm
Responsible for
For sending us off this cliff
And I'm pulling on the wheel and pulling on the wheel and the car is skidding
And we're Off
Off the edge
And there is n o t h i n g
Nothing but air
And in that moment
I know it's all my fault
And I know there's no going back
And I have to come to terms with everything
Everything
i have ever done and not done
And I feel
<It's weird>
But I feel

at peace

Because
I have to be
there's no other choice
And if you have to choose,
I mean
Isn't it better to choose
peace?

<...>
There is this guy
I don't know why I thought of this-
In Japan
-This is true-
There is this guy in Japan who rents himself out
To do nothing
He accompanies people, pretends to be a family
member or a date or whatever
But he also just-
Sometimes he just sits with people and reads Manga
while they work
Says goodbye to them on a train platform, takes a walk
with them in the park
And

I kinda wanna do that
Maybe not forever
But it'd be nice
If

I dunno
If I didn't have to -
If I could
Just
Be here
With someone
And
Just be me

## VAN GOGH

People don't want *art*!

They want product
and plastic
And propaganda

They want
-I dunno -
Cheap Home Renovations
And Parenting Hacks
and Muffin Recipes with Hidden Nutrients
And
and Storage Ideas for Small Spaces
and Muddy Toddlers Carrying Inappropriate Animals in from Outdoors:
        *What's that, sweetie? A squirrel, a gopher, a baby skunk?*
        *Oh, isn't he darling?*

Or they don't
They don't know *what* they want
And so they search and they search and they search,
but what they are searching for
Is
Already there
It's *inside*
*Inside them*
And it's rotting
It's rotting with
Every. single. moment. they are ignoring it

And feeding it Drek

And when they stop
When they stop the endless treadmill of
JUNK
You know what they stop on?

In a world of Big Thinkers
Of Incredible Creators
And Masters of Craft and Form and Skill
Of Linguists and Maestros
Of Virtuosos and Sages?

A hamster video
It's a hamster
Inside a cardboard box

It's elaborate
I mean, it's an elaborate hamster set up

It's an *Indiana-Jones*-level set up
With cardboard boxes
Like ALL the cardboard boxes
-Possibly ever created

And the little hamster is wiggling his little nose
And he's gotta get through this maze
And there's music:
Like <sings dangerous music>
<dangerous music starts>
<becomes the hamster>

And it starts simple enough
He has to weave through passages,
Slip through a slinky

There are little matchstick barricades
- and straws
He's gotta duck and jump over straws and pipe cleaners

And then it gets harder
There are levels, see?
Pringles containers to sneak through
And crumpled cut up paper
He lands in little vats of stuff, like
Ball pits of paper
and has to claw his way out

At one point there are these little blue styrofoam balls
They pour out of a hole in the maze wall and he sneaks inside the hole
And then you can see, he's like
*Oh shit*
*Bad idea*
And he comes right out
And it's like:

> We're on the Titanic
> <music shifts>
> And the water is coming in
> The water is pouring out of the hole
> He's gotta get out
> And he's eating -

I think he eats some of the styrofoam to get out
Or by mistake
I don't know what he's thinking at this point

But I'm thinking:
*Is this fun?*
*Was he ever having fun?*
*What am I watching?*

And then things get real:
Like <sings scarier music, like Carmina Burana>
The maze starts to move
There are blades covered in Blood
And like
Spiky things coming outta nowhere
Moving walls
If he had a tail
His tail woulda been cut off by now from the moving walls

And yeah it's all cardboard and toothpicks and nail polish
But HE doesn't know that
He's all
<Scamper scamper>
His little nose working the whole time
His little claw feet navigating falling bridges
And tunnels with like
plastic spiders the size half dollars
And decoupaged Dead bodies
And rotting rubber skeletons

And every time you think, *he's made it!*
*He must be done!*
There is Another level
He's always Leveling up
The music is always getting more stressful and terrifying
I mean
*Are they gonna feed him to a cat at the end or something?!*

WE DON'T KNOW
ANYTHING COULD HAPPEN
WHAT AM I DOING WITH MY LIFE

And i realize:
I AM THE HAMSTER
I have ALWAYS BEEN THE HAMSTER
I am always leveling up
But instead of things getting easier
They get harder
The game gets more complicated, more dangerous
There are Spikes and falling Objects and Monsters on all sides
>Are the monsters real? I don't know. It sure FEELS like they are.<
And the music keeps getting
WORSE

*<Music cuts out.*
*Sudden silence.*
*Stillness.>*

When Van Gogh painted sunflowers, no one was interested.

When he was institutionalized, he created "Starry Night" from the nighttime view from his asylum window.

He only sold one painting during his lifetime
and died poor.

127 million people have seen that hamster navigate a cardboard maze.

Do you still think they really want art?

SOLOMON

No I won't. That's you.
I'm not like you.

Not really.
A little bit, maybe.

Sometimes it feels like I *am* you.
And there's no other choice
It's predestined
Preordained:
    I will become you
But I-
I don't want to be like you.
Not that there's anything wrong with you.
It's just that there are so many things that are wrong with you.

You know who you are?
You're Abraham.

In the Bible.
Ever read it?
Me neither.
But the story goes that God tells Abraham to cut his son in half. And Abraham is like,
*Word up, God! Bet!*
And he is ready to cut his son in half but then God is like
*Whoa, dude! I wasn't serious. That was just a test to see if you were a jerk and guess what... you are.*

Or. Wait. That-
That story might have been about Devotion.
I think it was the other -
The other story about the king and the people arguing about a baby

Yes, yes.

There were these two women
Arguing that a baby was their baby, right?
And they go to the king
And the king, in all his wisdom, says *Okay, we'll just cut him in half and you can each get half of the baby*
And the one mother is like, *Great idea, shared custody*!
But the *true* mother is like, *I will give him up to let him live!*

And then the king - King Midas maybe?
But I don't think it was King Midas because he was the one who turned everything to gold including his daughter- *spoiler alert* - it did Not work out well for him

So then the King, who was noble and like the kind of king you want in charge, I mean, if you have to have a king,
SOLOMON!
It was King Solomon!
King Solomon says, *Mother who gave up the child so he could live, the child is clearly yours because you have his best intentions in mind - basically, not splitting him in twain.*

Seems like a low bar.

<> But maybe it's not.

You can't split everything in half
Not everything can break apart and still survive

*Picks up the book. Places it in front of Van Gogh.*

And some of us?
Some of us would rather let something go if it means it will live.

*Solomon exits, leaves Van Gogh with the book.*

*Franz enters.*

FRANZ

I made a thing!
I made an amazing thing!
I made an amazing thing that no one has ever made before!
You are going to freak out at this thing I made!

It's a thing that I made and when you see it, It'll be like someone unscrewed the top of your head, blew on your brain, then screwed the top of your head back on again. That's how crazy the thing I made is!

*Pause.*

Do you want to see the thing?

*Pause.*

Do you?

*Van Gogh shrugs.*

Okay! I'm gonna go get the thing!

*Starts to exit.*

Are you sure you want to see the thing? It's a pretty awesome thing. I don't want your mind to be so blown by the thing that it causes permanent damage. So are you sure?

*Van Gogh reluctantly nods.*

Okay. I'm gonna go get the thing!

*Van Gogh gets an idea, pages through the book. Finds THIS text inside the book.*

*Franz returns.*

*Van Gogh mouths some of the following text with Franz.*

I don't think you're ready to see the thing. I know what you're thinking! You're thinking "You didn't make a thing!" But that's not true! I made a thing! I thought about it! I imagined it, I figured out how to make it and I created the thing!

*When Franz approaches, Van Gogh abruptly closes the book.*

Okay
To be honest,
I'm a little scared to show you the thing.

'Cause here's the thing about the thing.
It might not work, the thing. It might not.

It might be like a parachute suit. I mean…it's not a parachute suit. But –
Have you heard about the parachute suit?

Franz Reichelt, yes!

That's who built the parachute suit.
He was French. Lived in France.
He was a tailor. Fixed people's pants. Also built the parachute suit.
>This is real. This really happened.<
It was a suit for pilots that would turn into a parachute if they had to jump out of an airplane but didn't have time to put on a parachute. Not a bad idea. A little niche, but interesting, right?
They'd get into the air and it would turn into a parachute and they'd float effortlessly down to the ground.

But he had to test it. So he went to the police and he said "I have to test my thing!" And they said "How?" and he said "by jumping off the top of the Eiffel Tower!" And they said "Are you drunk?" but they said it in French so it was "Tu es bourrée?"

And Franz said "Non, je ne suis pas ivre," which is obviously French for "No, I'm not drunk!"

Franz wanted to show his thing to everyone! Then, finally, on February 4, 1912, he got permission to jump off the Eiffel Tower.
Really. He did.
This happened.

His friends tried to talk him out of it but Franz said "Don't try to talk me out of this, friends! I made this amazing thing and it's going to be beautiful." But he said it in French. Probably. I mean, I don't know.

So he went to the first platform of the Eiffel Tower wearing his parachute suit. You ever see the first platform? It's high. Higher than you are thinking. It's not a first anything. There were movie cameras. Hundreds of people gathered to watch Franz leap from the tower and float effortlessly to the ground.

And when you see the film, there's-
There's this moment in the film
where he's not sure if he should jump. You can tell he's thinking "What if I'm wrong? What if my thing is a failure?"

But Franz leapt.

Franz plummeted fifty-seven meters to the ground.
That's 187 feet.
That's approximately the height of a 16-story building.

The parachute didn't slow his descent at all. Not even a little.

There was a big poof of dust.
Franz died instantly.

*During Franz's monologue, Van Gogh pages forward in the book and sees that Franz will eventually gain the courage to show the "thing" if Van Gogh relinquishes the book.*

As you can imagine, it really cast a pall on the afternoon.

And when you know
when you Know what's going to happen, you want to yell, "Franz, don't jump! You'll die! Franz, ne saute pas, tu vas mourir!"

But no matter how many times you watch the film and wish he won't jump…Franz jumps.

What if
What if my thing is like the parachute suit?

## WILD CHILD

I'M SO ANGRY.

But I don't
I don't want to be this way
I don't *wanna* be angry, don't you see?
I wanna be
Easy. I want everything to be
Easier. Everything feels like an emergency.
Doesn't everything feel like an emergency?!
          Look at my eye
It's swollen, right? What Is That?
And my back
My back just started spasming outta nowhere today
Like it like it like it
Didn't want to be a part of me anymore
It wants OUT of my body
My body wants out of my body

It's all this
-Stress-
Stress isn't a big enough word
It's like, my body is manifesting all of the Emotional
Angst of the Entire World
And it's punishing me with it
It doesn't matter how well adjusted I try to be
Or how Pleasant I am
Or how Calmly I try to deal with
E V E R Y T H I N G

It's like
It's a - parasite - no, that's not the word

It's like
-an Infection

The Stress is an Infection and it's taking over my body
And now my body is Rebelling
And trying to get Out of my body

And I cannot help but DESTROY EVERYTHING

I wanna
I wanna
<howl>
<howl>

Oh wow, that feels good. Try it.

*FRANZ is hesitant.*

No really, try it.

*Franz tries a meager howl. Then WILD CHILD howls, then Franz, then back and forth until they are creating a howling song. They stop.*

Have you heard of the wild child?

Memie Le Blanc - The Wild Girl of Champagne.

She lived for ten years in the forest
Until she was captured by the villagers of Songy in 1731.
After raiding an apple orchard dressed in rags.

She actually fought the villagers with a large wooden club.
One of the village noblemen told a bunch of hunters
"Capture her!"
So they did.
There are interviews.
Biographies.
But none of them say whether or not her capture was a good thing

What if Memie was just fine in the forest?
Living with the animals.
Fighting with a club.
Raiding the orchards.

No one questions it.
Instead, they say "Memie still learned to read and write!"
She lived to be very old
She even became wealthy!

But what if that's not the point?
What if the point is just....(can't find the words)
<howl>

And there are others - Victor of Aveyron, Kamala & Amala in India, Marina Chapman in Columbia.
There are children who were
Literally
raised by wolves.

Or animals. They survived in the wild. Alone.
Abandoned.
From infancy, some of them.
How did they -
<>
I know I'm not alone. Not exactly.
But I can't help but feel like no one is coming.
No one is coming to save us.

## JOSEPHINE

"Inspired lists of valuable efforts yield open understanding."
What–
What does that mean?
"Inspired lists of valuable efforts yield open understanding."

Do you know Josephine Baker?
Not personally, I mean,
-from history.
You probably know her from the banana skirt.
She took vaudeville by storm.
Born in St. Louis, became the toast of France.
1500 marriage proposals - that's what they say
She received 1500 marriage proposals.
Could you imagine?
She adopted children from all over the world - 12
12 children!
She called them her Rainbow Tribe
To show that people from all over the world could live and grow together in peace
That's how she created her family.
And she-
During the war, the second world war
She smuggled messages for the French
through invisible ink in her sheet music
She sent messages in code.

Cause no one expects a performer to do anything but
entertain

I think about her sometimes.
It's funny what we remember about a person.
She was the only woman to speak at the March on
Washington in 1968
And she received the highest medal of honor for her
service to the French during the war.
"Inspired lists of valuable efforts yield open
understanding."
All people think of is the banana skirt.

GOODY PROCTOR

It will be okay?!

People are being Murdered in the streets
Women dragged into Unmarked Cars
Taken away from their families
-Children-
The Elderly
I am afraid to come here
To this place
I am afraid to go anywhere
It's like my whole system is on high alert at all times
DINGDINGDINGDINGDING:
Dangerdangerdangerdanger

*Tremor. Books fall from shelves. It's as if the library is part of Goody.*

I have to force myself to breathe
It's like my body forgets how

<deep breath in, out>

I was driving the other day
The other day i was driving along
And I saw this Lump on the side of the road
And I was like
"Ohmygod that's a dead body"
And it didn't phase me
I mean, it phased me but also
It was my first thought

Why was that my first thought?

> Oh, look, a lump on the side of the road:
> A dead body

...

It was a heap of trash

*Another tremor. More books fall from shelves.*

When they were burning witches
At the stake
Like in the 1600s
- No, sorry, -
I mean: women
When they were burning *women*
At the stake

They burned *women*
Not witches

It was dark, right? No electricity then
And people - they didn't have eye exams like we do
I mean, how many people do you know that wear glasses, right?
And so lots of people are stumbling around in the dark times
With poor eye sight
And so they saw things
In the dark
Plus the devil was Everywhere

I mean, not like a lot of entertainment options in the 1600s, you know
It was like…I dunno
Church and Executions and… Animal-baiting
So you could see why they'd be stressed out

*A larger tremor. More books fall.*

And there's that play
We read it in high school
The one with the, um, the
*"I saw Goody Proctor with the devil and I saw Goody Corey with the devil"*
And when i was reading that play
I was walking home from school
And I glanced down
And there was a dead crow under a tree
A dead crow
And I thought, *wow, it's everywhere*
*The devil* **is** *everywhere*

Then I did a double take:
It was just an old black work glove.

Something horrible is going to happen.
Something horrible is going to happen.

MARINA

You don't have to say anything.
You can just nod.

You don't even have to nod if you don't want to.
We can just be here with each other.
<....>

Sometimes
Sometimes I feel like I have to
Do something, say something, be somewhere
or it means that I'm not
I dunno.
Enough. I'm not Doing enough.

But that's not true.
I have to tell myself, everyday I have to
Remind myself:     That's     not     true

And in time-
When I Don't do anything

Or Say anything or go anywhere
In time I realize
What is true

<...>

There's this artist, you know her?
This, um, Yugoslavian artist

Who-
I don't think Yugoslavia exists anymore...

Well, she did this piece where she
She sat for eight hours a day
And made eye contact with strangers
When did she go to the bathroom I wonder
Or eat - Or
I mean it's not about that, but also these are the things I think about-

The point is
The point is:
people would sit for
Minutes
Hours
And just
<>
Three months, almost every day, eight hours a day
Over *700* hours
Of
Being
Present

...

What, has it been like,
a minute?

I think
It makes us uncomfortable.
The quiet.

<>

Sometimes I feel the weight of grief in my solar plexus as if it's coming from inside me. Like it's the Nothing and it's going to swallow me from the inside out, transform me into something monstrous and savage, until I don't recognize myself. Until I'm nothing but grief. Sometimes I feel like I could cry until the end of time and it wouldn't be enough.

"Inspired. Lists. Of. Valuable. Efforts. Yield. Open. Understanding."

It's a code.

There are messages everywhere if you are willing to listen.